The Long, Dark, Scary Night

by
Pat Holt
and
Robyn Vander Weide

Illustrations by Monica Minto

For
every boy or girl who has been afraid,
needing both comfort and courage

Copyright © 2009 by Pat Holt and Robyn Vander Weide

THE LONG, DARK, SCARY NIGHT
by Pat Holt and Robyn Vander Weide

Printed in the United States of America

ISBN 978-1-60791-605-5

All rights reserved solely by the author. The author guarantees all contents are original and do not infringe upon the legal rights of any other person or work. No part of this book may be reproduced in any form without the permission of the author. The views expressed in this book are not necessarily those of the publisher.

Unless otherwise indicated, Bible quotations are taken from the New King James Version. Copyright © 1979, 1980, 1982 by Thomas Nelson, Inc.

www.xulonpress.com

A Personal Note to You

Dear Reader,

The Long Dark Scary Night deals with the issue of fear. The story was inspired by a young boy's fear of the dark. The boy gained victory over his fear by applying truth from God's Word. Whenever this story is shared in homes, schools, and churches, it helps boys and girls find victory over fear.

Overcoming fear with faith in God is the Biblical principle presented in this story, and is applicable in dealing with fears of all types. FEAR FIGHTS FAITH, BUT FAITH IN GOD WILL FIGHT FEAR.

Pat and Robyn are committed to providing stories that illustrate how the Bible can be applied in children's lives. Biblical principles are woven throughout each story. It is our prayer that, as you and your child/children read this story, it will be a time of learning, worship, and enjoyment.

Because of His Love,

It is nighttime. Outside all is darkness, and it's cold. Inside Dylan's house, the lights are on, and there is a fire in the fireplace. It is warm and cozy. Dylan is playing with his favorite train set.

Mommy and Daddy are reading.

"Why, it's getting late," Dylan's Mommy says.
"Time for bed, Dylan."

"Can I just stay up for a little while—please?" Dylan politely asks. "I need to add more tracks."

"Well... all right, Dylan," Daddy says with a smile. "You've worked so hard."

Now the truth is that Dylan doesn't want to go to bed. He is afraid of the dark. He is afraid of being alone in a dark room. All too soon, Mommy and Daddy tell Dylan that he must get ready for bed. Slowly Dylan undresses. S-l-o-w-l-y he puts on his pajamas.

S-L-O-W-L-Y he brushes his teeth. He does not want to go to bed.

Mommy and Daddy come in for a Bible story, and then they kneel for prayers.

They kiss Dylan good night. Then Mommy and Daddy say, "Good night. We love you," turn the light off, and leave the room.

Now Dylan is alone in a black room. He keeps his eyes wide open. He wants to be sure there is nothing scary in his room before he closes his eyes. He looks around, but he doesn't see anything scary . . . not yet. He peeks under the bed. That's where it is. Something shadowy and scary with big eyes and long teeth.

"It's a monster!" he screams. He jumps out of the bed and runs into the room where Mommy and Daddy are reading. "A monster! A monster!" Dylan screams.

"There is a real live monster under my bed, I can't sleep in there. I don't want to go back."

Mommy takes Dylan on her lap, and tells him not to be afraid.

After he calms down, Mommy and Daddy take him by the hand to his room, turn on the light, and look under the bed. Daddy laughs. "Here's your monster, Dylan," he says holding up Dylan's favorite stuffed animal dog, Racer.

Mommy giggles too. "Dylan, there is nothing to be afraid of. There are no monsters. Now get back into bed. Take Racer with you."

The inky darkness is all around Dylan. He hugs Racer close to him. He whispers to Racer, "I know God loves me, and I know Mommy and Daddy love me, but there still might be something scary here!" He looks under the bed. Nothing scary under there. "Phew", Dylan breathes. Then he takes a long look all around the room. "Oh, n-n-no!" Dylan stutters, holding Racer very tightly. "W-w-what's th-that c-c-climbing up the w-w-window? It's a d-d-dragon!" Dylan leaps out of his bed.

"A d-d-dragon!" Dylan yells, running to his mommy and daddy. "There is a dragon climbing up the window. Racer saw it too." He begins to cry.

Mommy and Daddy take Dylan back to his room by the hand, and turn on the light. They look on the window where Dylan is pointing. Sure enough, there is something moving up the window.

"Do you see it, Dylan?" his daddy asks.

"Yes," Dylan answers. "But what is it?"

"It's a shadow of a tree branch outside, moving in the wind, Dylan," his daddy answers. "That's all it is. Nothing very scary about a shadow of a tree branch is there?"

"No," says Dylan. "Not when the light is on, and not when you and Mommy are with me!"

"Dylan!" Daddy says, "God can help you not to be afraid of the dark. Let's pray to Him right now." So Dylan, Racer, Mommy, and Daddy all kneel, while Daddy prays that Dylan will not be afraid of the dark, and that God will help him get to sleep.

Then Mommy tucks Dylan and Racer into bed, kisses Dylan, and leaves, turning the light off.

"I guess we'd better get to sleep now, Racer," Dylan whispers. Dylan peeks out from under the covers. Everything seems to be okay. Nothing scary under the bed; or on the wall; or by the windows. Then he looks above the closet and sees a spooky ghost, looking down at him. It seems to be coming closer!

"Eeeeeeee!" Dylan shouts.

He throws back the covers, grabs Racer, and runs as fast as he can. "Help! Come quick! There is real ghost in my room, getting closer and closer to my bed."

Mommy and Daddy hurry into Dylan's room to see the ghost. But in the light they look up. Instead of a ghost, they see a shirt hanging above the closet.

Mommy chuckles.

Daddy also smiles. "That isn't a very frightening ghost, is it, Dylan?"

"No, Daddy," he admits.

"Sit down on your bed with Mommy, Dylan," Daddy says, as he leaves the room. When he comes back he is holding his Bible. He sits down and opens his Bible.

"Dylan, is there really anything in your room to be afraid of?" he asks.

"Well... er... uh... no, Daddy. But I can't help it. I'm afraid. I just am afraid of the dark," he answers.

"I know you are," Daddy says. "Would you be afraid if Jesus were here with you?"

"Oh, no," Dylan answers. "Because He could take really good care of me."

"Dylan, right here in the Bible," Daddy says, pointing to Matthew 28:20, "there is a verse that tells you that Jesus is with you even in a dark room with the lights out."

"Is that what it really says?"

"Listen to the Bible verse. Jesus says 'I am with you always.' Does that mean Jesus is with you, even when it is dark?"

"Yes, I guess so. Daddy. But I can't see Him."

"I know that Dylan. But is He with you in a dark room?"

"Well... yes."

"Of course, He is. Now you say it."

"Jesus is with me always."

"Is the Bible true, Dylan?"

"Oh, yes," Dylan answered.

"Then you can really believe it when you say, 'Jesus is with me always,' can't you?"

"Even in a room with no light—huh, Daddy?"

"That's right, son. We are going to kneel by your bed again, Dylan, and I want you to ask God to help you to remember that Jesus is with you always— even when you are here at night."

"Okay, Daddy." They all kneel and Dylan prays, "Dear God, I know You love me and don't want me to be afraid of the dark. I know that Mommy and Daddy love me too. Help me to remember that Jesus is with me always—even in a dark room that seems kind of scary. Amen."

Then Dylan crawls into bed.

"Dylan, your mother and I want you to say that Bible verse over and over again to yourself, when we leave."

"Okay, Mommy and Daddy. I love you."

"And we love you," Daddy says, "and so does Jesus." Mommy and Daddy leave the room.

Dylan begins to whisper out loud. " 'Jesus is with me always,' " he says, looking all around. " 'Jesus is with me always,' " checking the walls, ceiling, and under the bed. " 'Jesus is with me always.' " Then Dylan snuggles on his pillow, closes his eyes, and falls fast asleep.

From that night on, Dylan remembered that Jesus is with him always—even in a dark room.

DID THE CHILDREN GET IT? Ask these questions.

The following questions complete this story lesson. Asking them will help you to know if the point of the story is understood so that your child/children can apply the Biblical principle in daily life.

The questions are arranged in order of the difficulty of thinking skills needed to answer them. For example, a "Recall" question is the easiest to answer; a "Synthesis" question is much more difficult.

At first, your child/children may only be able to answer one or two questions. Do not be discouraged! The mind is being expanded by the challenging nature of the questions. With greater understanding comes greater application. Help your child/children with the answers when necessary. After several readings, your child/children may be able to answer all the questions - and that's exciting!

Recall	"What was Dylan playing with?" His train.
Comprehension	"Why didn't Dylan want to go to bed?" He was afraid of the dark.
Application	"Have you ever been afraid of the dark?" (Child/children share.)
Analysis	"In what part of the story did Dylan stop being afraid of the dark?" When his mommy and daddy showed him the Bible verse that says, "You can be sure that I will be with you always."
Synthesis	"What might have happened if Dylan hadn't found out from God's Word that Jesus is with him always?" He might still be afraid of the dark.
Evaluation	"Do you think that Dylan will ever be afraid of the dark, as long as he remembers that Jesus is with him?" No.

Printed in the United States
144170LV00004B/1/P